THE ORTHODONTIC BLUEPRINT:

THE ULTIMATE GUIDE ON HOW TO

BUILD YOUR AUTOMATED PRACTICE

AND GET YOUR FREEDOM BACK

By Dr Aalok Y Shukla

Published in 2015 by Click Convert Sell

Copyright © Dr Aalok Y Shukla 2015

http://www.straightteethengineacademy.com/

London

About the Author

Dr Aalok Y. Shukla is the co-founder of Click Convert Sell and Elite Virtual Team, and the Clinical Director of I Love Straight Teeth in London.

For the past 16 years, Aalok has studied and reverse engineered all aspects of data-driven marketing and sales using his own practice as a case study. The outcome is a marketing system that allows business owners to leverage direct response marketing, automation technology, virtual teams & simple staff systems to enhance productivity and increase freedom in their businesses.

This marketing system is the same automated system tested to deliver over 180 brace starts a year to a small general practice.

This strategy-packed handbook will walk you through some of the key principles of marketing your dental practice. In it, you will learn how to:

- Find the right message
- Target the right market
- Identify the right medium to use to position yourself as a knowledgeable authority and attract your ideal patients, and
- Automate the marketing system so it works without fail to bring in new braces patients without introducing more tasks to your to-do list

The strategies and tactics in this book are lifted directly from the marketing system that serves as the curriculum for The Straight Teeth Engine Academy. Read this book and implement the strategies inside. Your practice will never be the same again.

Contents

Introduction

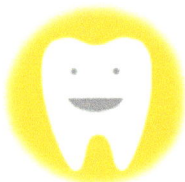

Most dentists and orthodontists go into dentistry for one very important reason: To help improve the lives of those around them. Too often it's the case that after starting your practice, the bills roll in and you have to shift your focus from transforming smiles and making people feel good about themselves to bringing in enough patients just to make sure there's enough income to cover your expenses. The entire process can be quite frustrating.

If this is your story, let me first tell you that I understand. I've been where you are. I know what it is to go to bed tired and wake up tired. I know how one can struggle to service more patients than it seems time will even allow. I understand what it feels like to labour day after day wondering if the patients I really want to see will come in to see me today.

Five years ago, my professional life had settled into a stubborn routine. I worked very hard for far too many hours and earned enough to cover expenses. Sound familiar? By no means was I lacking, but I wasn't satisfied with the way my practice was going. I wasn't seeing the patients I had envisaged seeing when I set up my practice. Yet I was working nonstop it seemed. I knew something had to change, I had to change.

What I had to finally reconcile is the fact that marketing is a non-negotiable part of managing a successful dental practice. I had to master the strategies that would help my practice attract teeth straightening patients on a daily basis, not every now and then.

I will teach you the basics of a complete marketing system. This short handbook will help you take the first important steps toward reshaping your practice. You know, for many of us, it's not just about landing more sales or boosting profits (though those two benefits certainly serve as fantastic byproducts). It's about living out a desire to use the skills you honed and the techniques you worked years to perfect to make people happier.

The marketing system I will show you does three things very well. It:

- Gives you back your time by teaching you how to outsource tasks to your virtual team and automate your marketing efforts
- Provides you with the flexibility and freedom you always wanted by allowing you to swap out your lower-value, time-intensive procedures for higher value treatments that take less time and effort
- Gets you back in the business of doing what you love and out of the habit of just doing what you *have* to do

In the next few pages, we will address several of the most common challenges my colleagues and I faced when we were overworked, frustrated and looking for a better way to do business.

I invite you to use the information I am going to share with you to create and implement a fail-proof system that will automatically send well-qualified, high-value potential patients your way. The marketing strategies in this book will enable you to accomplish more fulfilling work in less time and with fewer resources.

Let's get started.

I'm a fantastic dentist or orthodontist. So, why am I struggling to bring in patients?

As dental experts, we work extremely hard to gain the knowledge and develop the techniques needed to serve our patients. But we often overlook one key area of our own success and that's the fact that when we open our doors, we are no longer just doctors; we become business owners.

Most dentists are what I like to call "accidental business owners." I say that because whether or not you have a full lobby today, dentists are highly sought-after professionals. The reason we sometimes don't have the patient list we want when we first start out is because we have not learned how to properly market ourselves.

For good or for bad, dentists and orthodontists have a tendency to think that by developing their skills, they "earn the right" to win patients. Unfortunately, just being great at what you do is not going to compel a potential patient to give you a call. My friend, that is simply not the way this business works.

Being a skilled dentist does not beget a waiting room packed to the rafters with high-value patients. As dental practitioners, not only should we work on technique, but we must also develop and implement business strategies that will help us bring our ideal patients through the doors. And we have to find a way to do that using as little time, money and human capital as possible.

Doesn't seem like the easiest task to execute, does it? It's not that hard when you have a system in place that will help you streamline the process of targeting and acquiring new patients.

Now, if you start to feel yourself resisting my message, I want you to consider this: If you are constantly spending time and money in an effort to learn everything you can about the practice of orthodontics, you are probably looking to master your craft. But what good are your skills if you do not also take the time to build a system that will help you find and connect with the patients who will appreciate your hard work and take advantage of what you have to offer?

Imagine how much more enjoyable your days would be if you could invest the majority of your time and abilities doing the kind of work you like instead of laboring to get new patients in for any and every kind of treatment.

Do you have a marketing plan in place?

Most successful businesses operate based on a business plan. A business plan is not a new concept. Even if you didn't write one to open your practice, the chances are pretty good that you know what a business plan is and you know what it does.

A business plan identifies your company's mission, message and goals and outlines a detailed plan for how your company will fulfill its mission, share its message and reach its goals.

Why is this important? A well-written business plan provides you and your team with a roadmap that ultimately determines how you behave in the market. Your mission helps your team and your patients understand why your practice exists in the first place. Your message articulates the one or two potent ideas you want the world to know about your business. Your goals determine whom you serve and how you serve them.

Let's look again at the goals - whom you will serve and how you will serve them. In order for your practice to function the way you want it to function, you will have to identify your target potential patient and lay out the specific actions you will take to find and acquire them. This section of the business plan is called your marketing plan.

So, here's the big takeaway from this section: If you are struggling to bring in your ideal patient, your problem is probably not the quality of service you offer. Therefore, you will not fix your problem by improving your skill set. Your problem is most likely with your marketing plan. Take a look at how you crafted and developed your plan, and how effective you are at implementing your it.

No marketing plan? No problem.

Whether you need to retool your current marketing plan or you have to build one from scratch, this book is for you. The techniques that I present throughout this book are designed specifically for dental practitioners, to help you transform your practice into a highly productive, patient-attraction machine. And it won't cost you your weekends to get it done.

In fact, you actually don't need much marketing savvy at all. You just need to know and understand a handful of important concepts. The Straight Teeth Engine Academy marketing system will handle the rest.

I feel like I'm stuck on a treadmill instead of building. I'm barely making enough to pay my bills and my staff. Quite honestly, we have to take whatever patients we get and I'm losing my passion.

Many dental professionals end up having to endure a similar fate, sometimes for years before they are able to make the shift in their business. Trust me when I tell you that the cycle of labouring just to cover expenses is one of the primary causes of burnout in our line of work.

You may be tempted to fortify an already strong work ethic, put your nose to the grindstone, and keep at it with the hope that your diligence and hard work will lead to a fantastic breakthrough. But what sort of breakthrough, what sort of change can you expect if you continue taking the same course of action, day in and day out? The answer is none.

It's counterproductive to continue doing the same things over and over again, expecting a different outcome. I believe this wholeheartedly. You cannot lead change by conforming to the status quo. If your status quo has been working to earn a living instead of working to make a difference, it's time for you to embrace change.

Change the way you see things

The good news is you can change everything with just one good decision. If you are going to reshape your practice, you have to accept the fact that you can! Your business is not some mighty machine already in motion that you are unable to stop.

Whatever your practice is or isn't is the direct result of the steps you have taken thus far to fulfill your mission, spread your message and accomplish your goals. The moment you lose sight of even one of those three important factors is the moment your dental practice will start to get away from you.

That's not to say that we don't make sacrifices as health care providers. We do. It comes with the territory. But as business owners we also have goals that we want to see come to pass.

I would venture a bet that most dentists & orthodontists spend more time doing procedures and seeing patients that they would rather not see. That means less time doing what they love, which is straightening teeth and starting braces.

You may say, "I'm doing well enough. And we have to keep the bills paid after all." Sure, but remember, you are a limited resource with a finite amount of time and energy. Each time you have to take a job that you don't want to do in order to keep things afloat, you lose a little bit of yourself and a little more of your freedom.

If you want to get out of the rut in which you may now find yourself, first dispel the myth that "well enough" is good enough. It is not. Then put together a strategy to change things so you can grab the reins of your dental practice once again and start getting your time, energy, passion and life back.

Focus on boosting productivity

Productivity is the rate at which you are able to repeatedly invest your limited resources for the most gain. As you increase your productivity, you increase your freedom.

For orthodontists, higher-value patients produce the most professional benefit and are therefore a more productive use of your resources. For every hour you spend starting braces, for instance, your financial return and your emotional return are much higher than they are when you spend the afternoon servicing hygiene patients. After all, as an orthodontist, you have already invested a substantial amount of your own resources learning how to help people straighten their teeth. It would be a shame to work day after day and not get the opportunity to focus on your specialty.

Fast-growing businesses are able to grow by 20% each year for three years in a row. The most effective way to grow your business is to service high-value patients.

Consider this: If you use your resources to add 20 new hygiene patients to your patient list this year, you can probably expect to add £1,300 in revenue, assuming each new hygiene patient brings in £65. On the other hand, if you use those same resources to attract 20 new braces patients, you can expect to add about £40,000 in revenue.

So then, understanding that you have limited resources, which type of patient would offer the greatest return on your investment? The answer is obvious, isn't it? If you tailor your marketing efforts to attract higher-value patients, not only will you immediately boost your sense of accomplishment and fulfillment, you will greatly impact your bottom line. From here on out, we will deal specifically with bringing more high-value patient to your practice.

Zero in on getting those higher-value patients

Now let me ask you a key question: Who are you targeting right now with your marketing efforts? And who are your ideal patients? Everything you do from this point forward should be designed specifically to attract your target patients. In order to do that, you must have a clear picture of who your target patients are.

Are you targeting busy mothers who are somewhere in the process of researching teeth straightening for their children?

Perhaps you plan to target mature CEOs and influencers who are of a certain position in their companies or communities.

What about a bride-to-be preparing for her big day or an aspiring actor whose career is quickly gaining momentum? Both the bride and the actor need their teeth straightened quickly… and quietly.

Consider a young woman who is just starting her career. She had done the research and knows straightening her teeth is going to require her to quickly start redirecting funds to her "Rock Star Smile Fund."

Each of the above five potential patients has a different profile and with varying internal and external influences motivating their decisions to straighten their teeth. This is important to note because in order get their business, you are going to need to understand how to get their attention.

So, let's do a quick exercise: Think about the profiles of the five potential patients listed above. Why are they interested in braces? What do you think are their motivations? What are some of the obstacles they have to navigate that, if not resolved, may keep them moving forward and starting braces?

Let's look at the mother first. She is probably in her late thirties and responding to a request from her oldest child to get braces. The mother is more than willing to oblige as long as the process doesn't require the child to miss school and the mother to miss work.

The young woman starting her career could be looking to fine tune her professional brand to help with her upward mobility. But braces are expensive for a young and talented content strategist. She's worried she may not be able to afford braces right now.

What about the other three potential patients? What do you think are their motivations? What are their fears? When you can pinpoint who it is you want to target and identify both their desires and their fears, you can create a marketing funnel to attract them. We will deal more with developing that skill in later sections.

Work. Work. Work. I'm far too busy and I'm overwhelmed! How will I be able to finally attract the braces patients I want to see?

Why, that's the dream, is it not? Work the hours you want to work and see only the patients you want to see to perform procedures you enjoy performing.

I hope by now that you have it firmly in your mind that your skill and education have afforded you the opportunity to start a business that, if properly planned, can provide you with the freedom and financial resources to live the life you have always dreamed of living. There is only one thing standing between your current professional life and that dream life. That one things is a new and improved way of marketing your practice to draw the patients you want.

There is but one solution to your problem: Implement a marketing system

Sorry. There is no magic formula to boost sales without getting your hands dirty, so to speak. If your current marketing system (or lack thereof) isn't bringing you the right patient, you have to build a better system. You have to change something and change it now. You can plan this change step-by-step and implement it day-by-day.

While successful businesses can be automated, they are not automatic. In order for your practice to grow, you have to put a marketing system in place that fosters growth. Then you have to put people and procedures in place to oversee that growth so it has a positive impact on your business.

We work in a patient-facing industry. Your practice's most valuable assets will always be the relationships you are able to build - between you and your patients, between your patients and your team and between your team and you. It is in your very best interest to protect those relationships at all costs. The livelihood of your practice depends on it.

Still, you have to be careful not to overextend your staff. When your team members are overworked or worse yet, when they are dissatisfied at work, their ability to uphold the values of your practice are weakened. It gets hard for them to maintain a welcoming and stress-free work environment for your patients. So whenever possible, you want your patient-facing team members to focus solely on creating the best patient experiences they possibly can.

That is why we teach ambitious orthodontists to implement a marketing system that will funnel higher-value patients into their practices without putting an unnecessary strain on their staffs.

Implement a marketing plan that is targeted and precise

I know from experience that the thought of building a marketing system from scratch can be quite daunting. Where do you even begin?

Fortunately, you won't have to start from the beginning like I did five years ago when I was trying to figure out ways to target higher-value patients.

Let's first establish a basic truth: There is no such thing as a marketing campaign that appeals to everyone. In fact, the so-called machine gun approach to marketing typically doesn't get you any closer to reaching your ideal patient. It only uses up valuable resources. In order to be successful in your marketing efforts, you will need to create hyper-targeted messages for segments within your target audience.

A few pages back, I introduced you to five very different potential patients. If you noticed, they are all members of your target audience in that they all want braces. That is what they have in common and that is what makes them part of your target audience. But they all have different reasons for wanting braces because they are essentially using braces as a way to get straight teeth in order to accomplish some other goal.

One patient is concerned about landing more film roles. He wants to dash a dazzling smile as he walks down the red carpet. Another patient wants to provide for a child who, for whatever reason, wants straight teeth. Another wants her wedding day to be perfect and perfect teeth will help her to accomplish that goal.

So let's take two members of this group and compare their motivations and concerns.

The bride-to-be

The bride-to-be is racing the clock. She needs a solution that will accomplish what she needs it to accomplish without fail, and do so within a very specific amount of time. She wants a great smile for her wedding photos and she wants to look beautiful at the parties and events the week of her wedding. This includes the shaky Smartphone footage she knows her cousin will record of her.

She doesn't want a metal rack circling her mouth in the days and weeks leading up to her wedding though. She would like the entire process to be a bit more discreet.

She's is concerned about timing. She's concerned about not being able to enjoy the cake and food on her wedding day. It's a vague worry, but it's crossed her mind a time or two.

She is concerned about money too. The wedding is already pushing toward the very tiptop of its budget. And braces are a necessary expense in her mind. She doesn't want to be in and out of a dentist chair for the next few months. There's already just so much to do.

If she can skip over the part about wearing a retainer or anything like that on her honeymoon, that would also be quite fantastic. In fact, she's really only concerned with her big day. After that, she will deal with oral issues as they arise. If they arise.

The mother

The doting mother wants her son to have a positive experience at school. He's not dating yet, but that day is not very far off and if getting braces will help her boy to be more confident and sociable, the mother is all for it. Mum wants a permanent solution, though, if there is such a thing.

She understands there will be maintenance and maybe frequent office visits in the beginning. Not too frequent though. She doesn't want her son to miss too much school and she most certainly cannot afford to skip out on work too often. And the whole thing has to somehow fit around his football schedule and her younger daughter's ballet recitals. She's checked into it and braces are costly. Not first-car costly, but definitely winter-holiday costly. That concerns her, but she and the hubby can afford it. Still, she's searching for a doctor with a flawless reputation and great service at a competitive price.

Now that we know our two targets, answer a few quick questions for me:

- o Which of the two women would be more interested in picking up a handbook called "How to Get Straight Teeth in Time for Your Wedding" that talks about what you need to do if you want straight teeth in eight, six and four months?
- o Which of the two women would be swayed by a dental office that offered afterschool and weekend hours? What about an office that gave priority to school-aged kids during school breaks?
- o Which woman would be more interested in no-hassle options for straightening teeth?
- o Which would be more inclined to watch an informative video that offered an in-depth comparison of the three top teeth-straightening solutions that deliver the longest-lasting results?

Each of the four bullet points above represents a different piece of content. If you create great content for the wrong potential patient, it will not lead to more braces patients. But if you create the right content that markets your business to the right potential patient, you exponentially increase your chances of gaining that person as a new braces patient.

You now have a better understanding of why you absolutely must identify your target patient.

Create timely, relevant, interesting content

Your marketing plan has to be extremely focused on the needs, worries, challenges, desires and habits of the specific segment of the population you intend to target. As you can see just from comparing the bride-to-be with the mother, these two women have very different concerns and would be interested in consuming very different information.

There is no shortage of access to information in the Western World. Information is plentiful today and it's so easy to come by that no one is really impressed with general information anymore. **You have to specialise**. Just think about it. When these women go searching for a dental provider, do you really think they are going to go with a practice that categorizes itself as "general dentistry"?

No!

The bride is going to be on the hunt for someone who can straightened and whitened her teeth in one or two sessions and have them perfect for her in the next 180 days. The mother is going to look for a semi-permanent solution for her son's teeth. You can bet the dentist will be local, safe, friendly and open on the weekends.

Marketing is about crafting the **right message** to the **right market** using the **right media**. In the online world, that means you will be publishing fantastic multimedia content that your target audience wants and needs to get. And get ready because you will probably be producing quite a bit of it.

I have no time, I have no team, and I have no plan. How in the world am I going to make this all happen?

I can give you the answer in one word: Systems.

I will admit straight away that it's impossible for me to tell you everything you need to know in a 40-page book. Building a marketing system takes concise instruction, interactive learning, and hands-on experience, which is why The Straight Teeth Engine Academy exists in the first place. But for the sake of getting you started (and removing any opportunity you may have to use ignorance as an excuse to continue under-earning and over-performing), I will outline several key strategies over the next few pages.

Now, let's answer the question at hand.

Create a 12-month marketing plan

This actually isn't as complicated as it sounds. First of all, start your plan by identifying the patients you want to serve.

- o Who are they?
- o Where do they live?
- o What do they do for a living?
- o What things are most important to them?
- o Are they well-educated?
- o How much do they earn?
- o Who are their friends?
- o Where did they spend last Saturday?

Great marketers will tell you that whenever you write anything for an audience, you should write it to one person - that one person who typifies your target audience. It can be someone you know or someone you made up. Either way, you want to have that person firmly in mind when you write.

The same goes for you as you create your marketing plan. You need to know your target audience and you need to know them well. Just as we explored the psychology that motivates an engaged woman to suddenly get braces, you need to understand what drives your target patient.

Don't skip this part. Your marketing plan is non-negotiable. Besides, you already know what results you will get without a targeted marketing plan, which is why you grabbed this guide in the first place. You can't simply wing it when it comes to marketing your dental clinic and attracting your target patients.

Once you create your marketing plan, we can get to work implementing a marketing system that will deliver five to ten new braces patients **from your target demographic** to your dental practice each month.

Add a virtual team that will oversee your marketing funnel

Adding a virtual team to your practice is very important at this stage. It is your virtual team that will be in charge of overseeing your marketing funnel to make sure everything runs smoothly.

Your virtual team will be in charge of helping you:

- o Create multimedia content to attract potential patients
- o Manage your social media engagement
- o Develop an email autoresponder series that automatically sends a set programme of information to those who enquire
- o Relieve your on-site team of some customer service responsibilities so they can focus on building patient relationships in person
- o Direct patient questions to your staff for follow-up
- o Track the performance of your content to ensure those who seek you out are getting what they need from the content you publish
- o Maintain an interactive online relationship with potential patients

By outsourcing some aspects of your customer service and standardising some aspects of your marketing, you create an engine that will consistently grow your business. Excuses like, "I'm sick" are a thing of the past. You don't need to micromanage anyone. The engine you create just keeps going, the system keeps working. This automation/outsourcing strategy will also save your staff and your practice from being infected by office politics.

Getting a virtual team together is not difficult if you go with an agency. Employing the use of a virtual team will require an investment of about $500 per month. I highly recommend Elite Virtual Team (http://EliteVirtualTeam.co.uk). They offer a wonderfully-skilled pool of elite virtual assistants who can help you dream up and implement your marketing plan.

Another important point to remember is that while you may have one online team and one offline team, it's all one team. So make sure your in-house staff understands what the virtual team does and vice versa. The last thing you want to do is bring in a "virtual" staff and leave your regular staff in the dark. Not only can it cause confusion and provoke uncertainty and hostility within the team, but this lack of transparency can also result in duplicated efforts.

Make your vision and your goals clear to every single team member and align the responsibilities of the offline team with the responsibilities of the online team so everyone knows how and why the marketing system works.

Automate your marketing

The best thing you can do for yourself, your teams and your marketing efforts is to automate as much of your business as you possibly can. Your marketing system is only as strong as your willingness to rely on it. We will get more into this in the next section.

How do I attract my ideal patient without having to knock on doors or spend hours networking?

Target your marketing. The whole point of your marketing plan is really to identify the right message to share with your target audience. You should have a specific message for each segment of your target market that you are trying to reach. Create a strong message then use systems and virtual teams to automate the process of spreading that message to your ideal patient across every media channel they frequent.

Find the right media

In the online world, just as in the offline world, different clubs appeal to different types of people. If you quickly compare offline social clubs to online social media platforms, it may help you to understand what I mean. They have different users or members, different community cultures, different community rules, and different sets of best practices for engaging with one another.

In order to be effective in any one medium, you must first determine if your target audience uses that medium. If they do, you should adapt your message to fit that platform's distinct culture.

According to Pew Research Center - Internet, Science and Tech, women are the biggest Pinterest users by far. So if you are targeting men who are middle managers or C-level executives, your best options in 2014 were LinkedIn and Facebook. On the other hand, the mother from our earlier example is a good candidate for a platform like Pinterest. The actor probably spends a good portion of his social networking time searching for casting calls by frequenting Facebook's massive collection of media-focused groups.

Once you know where your target patients go when they come online, your job is to create and deliver your message using different types of media. While Facebook users may respond to memes and videos, people who use Instagram and Pinterest have gotten accustomed to communicating through images.

The core of your message will always remain the same. But in order to effectively engage your target patient, you will often have to change the way in which you deliver your message.

Shape your message to get attention

Once you have your message and you know where your ideal patients are hanging out online, the next variable is shaping and reshaping your message so it resonates with your ideal patient.

Here is how this plays out in the market: Let's say you are in the process of creating a campaign for competitively-priced invisible braces and you are targeting women in their twenties. The content you and your team create may be a slideshow with a survey component attached.

The headline your target will see online may read: "Which A-Lis Celebrity Has the Best Red Carpet Before and After Smile? (We're also going to tell you how much those pearly whites cost them)"

First of all, who wouldn't want to look at a slideshow of A-List celebrities? Second of all, the headline implies the publisher is about to reveal secrets the reader didn't previously know - young celebrities stars who have had work done. Already.

When your readers click the headline, the link will take them to a set of 8 to 15 slides, each with clear before and after pictures of celebrities they may know. At the end of the slideshow, readers get to vote on which star they think made the most positive transformation. Once they pick, a box drops down automatically to ask them if they are interested in knowing which products their celebrity choice used to achieve such stellar results. When they agree by adding their address and clicking submit, they get a second interactive slideshow that allows them to see the celebrity, their procedure and the price they paid to get it done. A cool twist would be to tell them the whopping amount of money the A-lister shelled out compared to the amount a regular person would probably pay to get the same results.

If you have properly targeted your audience, this presentation will end up in front of someone local who has been actively researching invisible braces. So this type of presentation would strike a chord with the reader. And since your target is in her twenties, you presented the information in a fun, shareable, interactive type of way.

The benefit to the reader is she gets tonnes of great information without having to search for it. And your practice gets one more opportunity to demonstrate its value to a member of its target audience.

No high-pressure sales tactics or boring scientific papers for them to read. Save the white paper for the CEO.

While your online efforts are invaluable, don't forget to include offline efforts as part of your marketing plan as well. If, for example, you are targeting a local community in which the residents are rather affluent, you may choose to put together a direct mail campaign.

You could send flyers or letters to their homes that direct them to your website to download an engaging, highly-valuable handbook of some sort, something that would really be of interest to them. It's really as simple as that.

Make time to build your online marketing plan alongside your offline marketing plan. Ideally, they should complement one another. Whether you first engage your targets online or offline, you will build the relationship online through email marketing and a varied catalog of entertaining information products like books, reports, images, videos, podcasts, websites, forums and social networks.

Ultimately, the goal is to move the relationship from their computer or mobile device to a face-to-face meeting. From the post box to the Internet to your reception area.

Create an engine that works around the clock to attract patients

By now, you have probably figured out why I say marketing is not easy. It's simple and straightforward - right message, right market, right medium - but not easy. Marketing is not a one-off event like a semi-annual white sale at the local department store. It is a system that will consistently push qualified potential patients into your network.

Attracting patients is a process, not an event. So plan and prepare for long-term success.

How can I use the Internet to build my dental practice?

In order to consistently grab the interest of your target market, you will need to use what's called a marketing funnel. A marketing funnel is an automated engine that works for you around the clock to attract customers. As you and your virtual team collaborate to create content, that content is used online and offline to get your potential patient's attention.

Sometimes potential patients will come across the content by chance. Other times, your content will show up in the results when they search for information about starting braces or straightening their teeth. The idea is that by providing your targets with enough useful information, strategies, tips and relationship-building opportunities your practices goes from being seen in their eyes as a helpful marketer to being seen as the most trusted name in your dentistry. And you're going to do all of this right online.

Use the Internet to segment your traffic

We've talked quite a bit about zeroing in on whom you really intend to serve. The way that you do that is by identifying the different segments of your market and creating content and programmes that are just for them. Again, not the easiest thing in the world, but the more you are able to segment your traffic, the more effective your marketing efforts will be.

Use the Internet to build your list of potential patients

Fortunately for dentists, creating targeted content, segmenting your traffic, and running automated marketing campaigns is the best way to build a list of well-qualified potential patients. I know from experience that receiving those weekly notifications of new leads is encouraging, especially when you build your first few marketing campaigns. When those leads come in, you already know that every new person on your list is a potential braces patient, not a hygiene patient or someone interested in bleaching. These are people who may come in to start braces this year!

Now, you should think of each different segment of your target audience as a separate list of customers who will experience their own special marketing campaign. So mothers get a special mothers-only campaign. Brides-to-be are showered with information about getting things done in the next 180 days. Influencers get the type of content that will engage them. Never mix your lists.

Why not?

Well, think about your personal life. In your personal life, you may bring your bookish friends together with your athletic friends for the occasional birthday bash, but just for general social activities, you probably keep those two groups separate because they have very different interests. It's the same with your lists. Whenever a potential patient grants you the privilege of access, you should honour that relationship well enough to keep him or her engaged with the types of content that you know engages the potential patient. Avoid luring potential patients into your funnel with specialty content then getting lazy about it and lumping them all together later on.

Use the Internet to build relationships

Once you have a potential patient in your marketing funnel, focus on engagement.

In this world of online dating and cyber friends, you may already be very skilled in the art of building relationships online. But I will offer this stern warning: Don't go right to the sell. The online relationships you develop with your future patients are just as delicate as the online relationships you may develop with a love interest or a colleague.

Take the time to prove you are valuable. It takes some doing to build a brand and it takes time for that brand to become trustworthy. People typically won't leave their health in the hands of a practice they don't trust.

Remember, I said your dental practice cannot survive without strong relationships. Well, strong relationships are based on trust. So whatever you did to get potential patients into your marketing funnel you will have to do the same and better to keep them there and eventually convert them to sales.

Help your patients understand the different procedures. Show them the difference between tradition metal braces and lingual braces or Invisalign. Show them in a quick video how to care for their braces. Tell them stories of when you had braces.

Later on, as your relationship matures a bit more and you see that your potential patient has opened your emails or asked questions in an online forum your team manages, forums, you can start adding a personal element to the relationship. Include things such as introducing members of your staff or giving subscribers a virtual tour of your practice. There is plenty of ground you can cover BEFORE asking for the sale. Each time you share your insights and demonstrate your value, you prove yourself trustworthy and prove that your practice is a place patients can come to get their issues resolved.

Use the Internet to manage your virtual team

Identify and communicate your expectations with your virtual team right from the start. That way, you can measure your team's performance by benchmarks and milestones, not by the fact that it's Monday, Wednesday or Friday.

If you took the time to build your 12-month marketing plan, it won't be hard to figure out where you are in the process and to measure your team's overall progress. In addition to using a virtual team, you will also have access to tools, processes and templates that help you to automate your marketing system. Automation makes it easier for you to assess your team's performance as you will know precisely what you're looking for after the third or fourth time checking their work. That's good news because it means you get to spend that time doing something other than fretting over their performance.

We already tried online marketing and advertising. It didn't work.

I actually hear this quite a bit from doctors who are either frustrated from ignorance or resistant to change. If you fit into either of these two groups, I can help you sort this out.

Why marketing efforts fail

If you really have spent time and money trying to generate leads with online marketing and your efforts haven't worked, I can guarantee you the problem is one of the following culprits:

- Either you don't have a clear message with an attractive offer
- You aren't targeting the market (the segmented lists of your ideal patient) with your message, or
- You are using the wrong medium or using the right medium improperly

We know the Internet is not broken. And according to a stat published on SmartInsights.com, 1.9 billion people will access the Internet with a mobile device this year, so the market is there. The problem then has to be in your execution.

One of the most common reasons why marketing efforts fail is because new marketers refuse to develop the patience to observe their market. They want to have these dry, one-sided online monologues. They want to create whatever they have the urge to create then blindly deem it worth for your attention just because they created it. They want to interrupt conversations already in progress on social media with "look at me!" ads. No one wants to be around a guy like that - online or offline.

Are you expecting total strangers to quickly convert to loyal patients? Why should they? What do they gain by listening to your sales pitch? Why would they choose you over another orthodontist that perhaps a friend can recommend. Speaking of, my best friend's band is now the house band on Thursday nights at Café Oto.

In the minds of your newest potential patients, there is very little to distinguish your dental practice from the one across town, or around the corner even. Your newest discount is not interesting! It's not valuable to them. You can't really consider it helpful information. It's not even news.

Question: Did you pause at all when I mentioned my friend's band? You may have wondered why I included that particular thought, but the fact that you made it down to this sentence lets me know that even if you did pause to wonder, you probably didn't bother to check Café Oto's website to find out about my best friend's band.

That's how people treat your content when you post statuses about discounts, sales and company news that only you care about. They may pause for a moment, but general information is *not* engagement, so they keep browsing the web.

Lack of real engagement is not relationship-building. Weak relationships may be why your marketing efforts have been unsuccessful.

And just so we're clear, I made up that bit about my best friend's band to prove a point.

People are reluctant to come in for treatment. How can I stand out from the crowd?

Your ability to tell your potential patients what is different about you is just as important as your need to create special marketing collateral just for the segments of your market that you have differentiated. If you want to stand out in a market brimming with qualified dentists and orthodontists, you have to separate yourself from the crowd.

Specialise

Brand positioning is very important to your overall professional brand. Brand positioning is the way in which you present your practice to the world.

For instance, a children's dentist may promote the fact that her practice is a safe and comfortable environment designed specifically for young children. Her staff members are patient and there is a spot in the examination area for parents to sit so a child can be comforted by being able to see his or her parents.

A dentist who specialises in restorative procedures, on the other hand, may focus on the fact that he delivers a pain-free experience and works with a team of porcelain crown experts who are unmatched in their ability to restore smiles.

Specialising helps your target audience to understand the one area of dentistry where you will display exceptional performance. People want that. When it's time for them to sit down in a dentist chair, they want the comfort of knowing that whatever happens - painful or pain-free - they are under the care of the best dental professional in town.

Professionals have a tendency to think that you reach the most people by advertising your services to everyone. In marketing, the opposite is true. Your goal is never to reach the most people. Your goal is to attract only your ideal braces patients. You can advertise to everyone and I guarantee you will grab more new hygiene patients than people who are ready to have their teeth straightened.

What you want to do is formulate your message so that your name, clinic, website, and content propel you to emerge as the most knowledgeable, most qualified, most authoritative expert in your region and on the web. You cannot do that by claiming to be an expert at general dentistry. "General dentistry" to most people means cleanings, fillings and x-rays.

Besides, if your braces patients had to choose between an expert and a generalist, they would go with the expert. Wouldn't you?

Double-check for consistency

This one is important. It's hard to find consistency anywhere these days. It's so rare, in fact, that thought leaders consider consistency a leadership trait. Consistency is the topic of articles in trade magazines. You can find quotes on consistency and memes about consistency because despite how important it is to your personal and professional success, it's just not that easy to come by.

When I use the term consistency, I am specifically referring to your willingness to completely conform to the application and implementation of the marketing system I put forth in this guide. Nothing else really matters if you are not willing to stick to this marketing system for at least 12 months. You can't have a short-sighted ethos and commit yourself to long-term strategies. The two conflict. So stop right now to check your professional life for consistency.

- o Are you creating the content you need to target multiple segments of your potential patient pool?
- o Are you creating enough content frequently enough?
- o Are you making sure your team follows up with any new leads?
- o Is your practice - the environment, the team, the technology, the expertise - consistent with the image your project?
- o Can you accomplish what your ads say you can accomplish?
- o Do you have a plan in place that covers your marketing TO DOs for one full calendar year?
- o Are you investing a sufficient amount of resources like time, attention and money to ensure your marketing strategy works?

I want you to quickly find and eradicate any dissonance between what you say you want and what your actions actually show. Train yourself and your staff to become beholden to your new marketing system no matter what.

Get help

You are about to embark upon a massive undertaking. It would take years for someone to create, implement, and test these strategies on his own. I know because it took me five years of consistently working at this to get everything all figured out.

Even with your virtual team in place, they will still look to you for direction, guidance and, of course, expertise. If you don't have it to impart, you may be signing yourself up to spend countless hours searching online for information that will help you connect the dots.

I strongly recommend you enrol in The Straight Teeth Engine Academy, a training programme I designed for dental professionals to help you navigate this ins and outs of managing this marketing system. Creating marketing collateral is one thing. Coming up with a marketing system that works is another. Now consider the fact that after you do all of the hard work to create the system, you will need to go back and teach your team how to implement it when you may still be learning it yourself. The Straight Teeth Engine Academy takes the guesswork out of your next twelve months of targeted marketing.

Learn effective systems and time-tested methods that work. Plus get access to a substantial catalogue of processes, templates and worksheets to help you build and oversee a marketing funnel that will work for you while you sleep.

The Straight Teeth Engine Academy is a twelve-month programme. That's the only way I could deliver all the necessary tools, resources and instruction for you in a way that is detailed and methodical without being overwhelming. When you complete this programme, you *will* understand your target market. But that's just the beginning.

You will add five to seven new braces patients every month just from your marketing efforts. Click here to learn more about this interactive new programme.

When you run a business, being able to get customers is the only thing that matters to your bottom line. You simply can't afford to let marketing be your blind spot.

Patients often know they need braces, but still don't get them. How do I close the deal?

First of all, don't panic. Your marketing system is designed to bring potential patients your way on a continual basis, so if a potential braces patient delays or decides not to continue on to start braces, expect another patient will be coming up right behind that one in just few days.

But to answer the question, this is actually where good The Straight Teeth Engine Academy training comes in handy. This particular problem cannot be solved with a quick marketing tip. It calls for sales training and scripts to help close sales.

I encourage you to enrol ahead of the next round of courses, which start the first Sunday of the month. You will be able to get the training you and your staff need to teach you how to convert doubts to yeses.

I do need help selling but I don't want to hire a sales team.

You will not have to hire a sales team. You won't need a single account executive. We have found a way to put you all in sales without making any of you a salesman.

Part of what The Straight Teeth Engine Academy does really well is help you to motivate your entire team to get new patients through the doors. We have a series of modules that teach team-building and sales skills.

We align the team with incentives, targets and rewards to help grow your practice. We help to ensure each team member is onboard with what is happening so the entire sales process is a win-win.

After going through our interactive training programme, your staff will have the skill set and the know-how to continue the sales process without having to resort to cold calling. When you enrol, we will teach you how to create warm leads on auto-pilot then we teach your team how to turn those warm leads into new braces patients.

What if I do all of this work and they still don't start braces?

You wait. Give your potential patients time to come to change their minds. Give them time to gather the resources and handle other logistical concerns. Give them time for this to become important enough and easy enough for them to act.

Most people are not going to say yes right away. What you want to do in this situation is to make sure you have your follow-up procedure in place.

Persist

While you wait, persist. Persist, but don't be pushy. People can refuse service for a number of reasons, but motivations change. Situations change. The thing that held your potential patient back from starting braces three months ago may no longer be an issue.

Most marketers will tell you, "The money's in the list." That means if you have targeted leads moving through your marketing funnel, it's only a matter of time before you make a sell. The more leads you have on your list, the more sales you make.

By the same token, sales professionals won't hesitate to tell you "The money's in the follow-up." That's because very often when a person says, "No" to something, it's actually more of a "Not right now." This is especially true if your leads have already demonstrated their interest in your products and services by agreeing to opt-in when presented with an opportunity to learn more from you via email. For you, the money is in both your list and your follow-up.

So when someone you thought would be a braces patient tells you no, that's your cue to put them into whatever marketing campaign you have designed specifically to overcome objections. More content, more media, a phone call here and there and an open invitation to come in and have their teeth straightened at some point in the future.

You may also want to:

- Develop and publish a series of video case studies of patients who have already had the procedure done
- Modify your email autoresponder campaign so that it's responsive. This allows future patients to tell you when to send more content and when to send less. This will also help you figure out where the person is in the decision-making process
- Continue building the relationship with small bonding gestures - personalising emails, publishing entertaining videos and images that include news about your local and virtual team members
- Send a text message twice a year to remind them when it's time for a dental checkup (and to help your orthodontic practice stay top-of-mind)

Delivering this kind of content can compel someone to stay in touch so when they are ready to straighten their teeth, your clinic is the first provider that comes to mind.

Address their concerns

This is a good time to systematically address all of their concerns. People love to buy, but don't care much for feeling as though they have been sold anything. So you should expect that there may be doubts lingering in the back of a potential patient's mind that they simply don't get around to vocalising. An unspoken doubt can impact a future patient just the same as an expressed doubt.

As part of your objection-overcoming content strategy, include blog posts, handbooks, Q&A webinars, one-on-one consultations and other media specifically created to address concerns and fears. Use every opportunity you can to engage your potential braces patient and quell his or her concerns.

Another good practice is to instruct every member of your team on how to answer some of the more common objections. That way whether the objection is being addressed using content, media or by an actual team member, the responses are consistent.

Future Patient: "It's too expensive for me."
> **Your message**: Well, here are our easy payment plan options.

Future Patient: "This is going to take too long. I don't know how I'm going to fit it in with work and the kids…"

Your message: We do offer weekend appointments and extended hours. We are open late every other Thursday.

Future Patient: "Is it painful?"

Your message: Here are some examples of people who have already had the procedure you will have. Here are their results. It doesn't really cause problems the way you think it may.

Future Patient: "I don't want to do it right now."

Your message: You may choose to wait, but waiting will definitely result in your teeth getting worse and you may not be able to get the same level of results.

Having scripted responses for overcoming objections is a good way to make sure potential patients have all the information they need to make an informed decision. You also serve them by warning them about the risks of waiting to get procedures done. When it comes to your oral health, there is an inherent cost to waiting. Make sure they know what waiting will cost them.

The marketing is working. What's next?

Fortify the relationship. From the moment new patients walk through the doors of your dental clinic, you and your team should make every effort to wow them. Give them the best experience possible. Prepare your office, prepare your team, prepare the waiting area. Everything about your office should reinforce the message that your patient has made the right decision by coming to you.

Create a comfortable office environment for offline engagement

In the waiting room, make sure your offline value matches your online value. Fill the waiting room with current magazines and quick reads on different procedures. Patients should feel relaxed and cared for. You don't want them to feel rushed, but you also don't want them to feel forgotten.

When your patients sit down with you, answer their questions and make sure you take the time to explain procedures clearly. The better they understand what outcomes to expect, the more they will trust your ability to deliver those outcomes.

Empower your patients

A good way to help new patients feel more secure is to provide them with options. Try to help them feel empowered about procedures by letting them know the options available to them and allowing them to choose. I always aim to provide my patients with three options and I respect their decisions.

Of course, as the expert, your patients will want to know your professional opinion on the best course of action, but keeping them actively involved in the decision-making process will go a long way toward building the doctor-patient relationship.

Dote on your patients

Once you get a new patient into the office, your primary focus should be optimising the patient's in-office experience. Let's talk about a couple of easy ways to show you care.

Aftercare. Invite your patients to take part in aftercare programmes. On a related note, whenever possible, try to be the very first call a new patient receives from your office after having a procedure done. Yes, it's easier to delegate that task but your patient will appreciate and *remember* your effort.

Care package. Before patients leave your office for the first time, load them up with oral hygiene goodies. This can be as simple as a toothbrush, toothpaste, floss and a mirror in a gift bag. The points is your patients will use their goodies and remember where they got them.

Reward referrals. In the weeks and months following your patient's teeth straightening procedure, things should be going rather well, well enough for you to ask for a referral. Whenever your patients send you a new braces patient, offer a handsome reward. Perhaps a weekend getaway or tickets to Disneyland Paris. Whatever the reward, make it memorable. You may spend a few hundred pounds, but the referral will be worth a few thousand pounds.

Stay in touch

Keep your customers in your funnel, segmented in a separate list just for current patients. Every now and then, send them more great information - interesting statistics, funny memes, more slideshow surveys, or other content you know they will appreciate. Keep strengthening your relationship because no business can ever have too many raving fans.

The Straight Teeth Engine Academy

Earlier in this book, I introduced a powerful resource to teach you how to implement a marketing system that will help your practice start another seven to twelve braces per month and add £100,00 - £300,000 to your practice.

What is it?

The Straight Teeth Engine Academy is a content-packed course that walks you through the process of building a marketing system for your practice that will help you attract a flood of new braces patients.

The marketing system I teach in the course - honed over more than 60 months of development, implementation and testing - has allowed my practice to generate more qualified braces patients than we can actually service. This is the same system we used to start 17 braces and schedule 42 braces consultations in a single day.

Since implementing the strategies and tactics of The Straight Teeth Engine, my staff and I have been able to significantly increase our bottom line while reducing the amount of work we actually have to do on a day-to-day basis. This is a brilliantly-designed, high-performing marketing system and I am extending an invitation for the most ambitious orthodontists out there who are serious about growing their businesses, not by 10% or 15%, but exponentially.

What will I learn?

I'm glad you asked that. The Straight Teeth Engine Academy is a 12-month programme that teaches you the four pillars of mastering marketing:

1. Attract Traffic
2. Build Patient List
3. Convert Sales
4. Deliver Wow

Each module works through hands-on learning. We are concerned with ensuring that with every new strategy or tactic you learn you are to immediately implement.

As part of the deliverables for this course, you will get access to actionable monthly strategies, goals and worksheets for your team; downloadable PDF course materials; monthly coaching call on latest practice ideas; motivational ideas; access to the STE Inner Circle where you can get hands-on advice; as well as templates for emails, guides and referral posers.

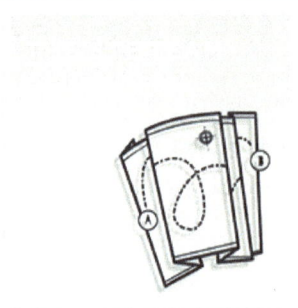

Learn which parts of your business to automate and which to outsource. Learn how to align your virtual team with your on-site team to perpetuate collaboration. Allow team members to train so they can learn how to support and become part of the sales process. When they complete the training, they will know just how to engage with your patients in a way that instills confidence and closes sales.

Enrol in this powerful training today by clicking here. The next session starts soon.

To get more information:

Visit our website at http://www.straightteethengineacademy.com.

Email your enquiry to hello@clickconvertsell.com.